EMMANUEL JOSEPH

Rare Diseases: Research and Support for Individuals with Rare and Often Neglected Medical Conditions

First edition

This book was professionally typeset on Reedsy.
Find out more at reedsy.com

Contents

1

Chapter 1: Introduction to Rare Diseases

Rare diseases, also known as orphan diseases, are a group of medical conditions that affect a relatively small number of people in the population. In this chapter, we will delve into the fundamental aspects of rare diseases, providing a comprehensive introduction to this unique and often overlooked category of medical conditions.

Defining Rare Diseases:
- What is the definition of a rare disease?
- Understanding the rarity threshold in different countries
- Rare diseases vs. common diseases – a comparative analysis

Prevalence and Significance:
- Estimating the global prevalence of rare diseases
- The burden of rare diseases on individuals and society
- Economic and social implications of rare diseases

Historical Context:
- A historical overview of rare diseases
- Pioneering discoveries and medical breakthroughs
- How the perception of rare diseases has evolved over time

This chapter aims to set the stage for the rest of the book by providing readers with a clear understanding of what rare diseases are, their significance, and the context in which they exist within the field of medicine.

2

Chapter 2: The Spectrum of Rare Diseases

Rare diseases encompass a vast and diverse spectrum of medical conditions, each unique in its presentation, impact, and underlying causes. In this chapter, we will explore the intricacies of rare diseases, categorizing them, highlighting common characteristics, and providing examples to illustrate the wide range of conditions that fall under this umbrella.

Categorizing Rare Diseases:

Rare diseases cannot be neatly classified into a single category. They can affect virtually any system or organ in the body, making categorization a complex endeavor. However, several broad categories help in understanding the diversity of rare diseases, including:

- Genetic disorders: These result from mutations or alterations in an individual's DNA and can be inherited or occur spontaneously.

- Metabolic disorders: These involve abnormalities in the body's chemical processes, often leading to the accumulation or deficiency of specific substances.

- Autoimmune diseases: In these conditions, the immune system mistakenly attacks the body's own cells or tissues.

- Rare cancers: Certain types of cancer are considered rare due to their low incidence, requiring specialized treatment approaches.

Common Characteristics:

Despite the wide-ranging nature of rare diseases, there are several common characteristics that many of them share. These characteristics include:

- Limited prevalence: Rare diseases are, by definition, infrequent within the population, which can lead to diagnostic challenges.

- High degree of complexity: Many rare diseases are highly complex, affecting multiple body systems and requiring specialized care.

- Significant variability: The presentation and progression of rare diseases can vary greatly from one individual to another.

- Genetic basis: A substantial portion of rare diseases has a genetic component, making genetic testing a crucial diagnostic tool.

- Often chronic and progressive: Rare diseases can be chronic and may worsen over time, posing ongoing challenges for individuals and their families.

Examples of Rare Diseases:

To gain a better understanding of the vast spectrum of rare diseases, let's explore a few examples:

- Cystic Fibrosis: This genetic disorder affects the respiratory, digestive, and reproductive systems, leading to thick mucus production and frequent lung infections.

- Huntington's Disease: A neurodegenerative disorder, Huntington's leads to cognitive decline, motor dysfunction, and emotional disturbances.

- Pompe Disease: This metabolic disorder results from a deficiency of the enzyme acid alpha-glucosidase and can lead to muscle weakness and heart problems.

- Systemic Lupus Erythematosus (SLE): An autoimmune disease, SLE can affect various organs and tissues, causing inflammation and a range of symptoms.

- Histiocytosis: A group of rare disorders characterized by the overproduction of white blood cells called histiocytes, which can accumulate in various tissues.

These examples highlight the diversity in rare diseases, both in terms of affected systems and underlying causes. Each rare disease comes with its unique challenges, treatment approaches, and support needs.

In the subsequent chapters of this book, we will delve deeper into the diagnostic, treatment, and support aspects of rare diseases, recognizing the importance of individualized care and research efforts in addressing these conditions effectively.

3

Chapter 3: Diagnostic Challenges and Advances

The diagnosis of rare diseases is often a complex and arduous journey, fraught with challenges and uncertainties. In this chapter, we will explore the intricate process of diagnosing rare diseases, the obstacles that individuals and healthcare providers face, and the advances that are revolutionizing the diagnostic landscape.

The Diagnostic Odyssey:

For individuals living with rare diseases, the path to diagnosis is frequently referred to as a "diagnostic odyssey." This odyssey is marked by a series of medical consultations, tests, and often, misdiagnoses before arriving at a conclusive diagnosis. It can be emotionally and physically taxing for patients and their families. This section will cover:
- The emotional toll of the diagnostic odyssey.
- The impact on healthcare resources and costs.
- The need for greater awareness and education among healthcare professionals.

Genetic Testing and Precision Medicine:

In recent years, the advent of genetic testing has been a game-changer in diagnosing rare diseases. Advances in genomics and the availability of whole exome and whole genome sequencing have allowed for more accurate and rapid identification of genetic mutations responsible for many rare conditions. This section will delve into:

- The role of genetic testing in rare disease diagnosis.
- The importance of precision medicine in tailoring treatments to genetic profiles.
- Ethical considerations and challenges associated with genetic testing.

Early Diagnosis Importance:

Early diagnosis of rare diseases is paramount, as it often translates to better treatment outcomes and improved quality of life for affected individuals. This section will emphasize:

- The impact of early diagnosis on treatment options.
- The significance of newborn screening programs in identifying rare diseases in infancy.
- The role of patient advocacy and awareness in promoting early diagnosis.

Undiagnosed Rare Diseases:

For some individuals, the diagnostic journey ends with an "undiagnosed" label, as the cause of their symptoms remains elusive. The frustrations and uncertainties faced by those with undiagnosed rare diseases are a crucial aspect of this chapter. We will discuss:

- The challenges of living with an undiagnosed condition.
- The role of research and collaboration in solving undiagnosed cases.
- Support networks and resources available to individuals with undiagnosed rare diseases.

This chapter will shed light on the labyrinthine path to diagnosis that many individuals with rare diseases traverse. It will underline the importance of early and accurate diagnosis, the role of genetic testing, and the significance of addressing undiagnosed cases. As we progress through the subsequent chapters, we will explore the evolving landscape of rare disease research, advocacy, and support, all of which are essential in improving the diagnostic process for rare diseases.

4

Chapter 4: Understanding Rare Disease Research

Research is the cornerstone of progress in understanding, diagnosing, and treating rare diseases. In this chapter, we will delve into the pivotal role that research plays in the rare disease community, exploring the various aspects of research, funding, and recent breakthroughs that are shaping the landscape of rare diseases.

The Role of Medical Research:

Medical research serves as the driving force behind our understanding of rare diseases. It encompasses a wide range of activities, from laboratory studies and clinical trials to epidemiological investigations. This section will detail:

- The pivotal role of research in uncovering the underlying causes of rare diseases.

- The importance of collaboration between researchers, healthcare professionals, and patient advocacy groups.

- The influence of rare disease research on our broader understanding of medicine.

Funding and Collaboration:

Rare disease research relies on financial support, often necessitating collaboration between government agencies, private organizations, and philanthropic efforts. This section will explore:

- Sources of funding for rare disease research, including government grants and private foundations.

- The need for international collaboration to pool resources and expertise.

- Case studies of successful collaborative research efforts.

Recent Breakthroughs:

In recent years, significant breakthroughs have been made in the understanding and treatment of rare diseases. Researchers have uncovered novel therapies, identified genetic mutations, and developed innovative diagnostic tools. This section will highlight:

- Recent examples of groundbreaking research in rare diseases.

- How these breakthroughs have transformed the lives of affected individuals.

- The promise of emerging technologies, such as gene editing and gene therapy.

Patient Involvement in Research:

Patients and their families play a critical role in rare disease research. Their insights, participation in clinical trials, and advocacy efforts can accelerate progress. This section will discuss:

- The importance of patient registries and data collection.

- How patient stories have led to research discoveries.

- Ethical considerations in patient involvement, including informed consent and privacy.

Challenges and Future Directions:

While significant progress has been made, rare disease research still faces numerous challenges, including limited resources and the sheer complexity of many conditions. This section will explore:

- Ongoing challenges in funding and prioritizing research.

- The potential for emerging technologies, such as AI and big data, to advance rare disease research.

- Future directions and the role of international organizations in coordinating research efforts.

Understanding rare disease research is vital for comprehending the ever-evolving landscape of these conditions. This chapter will underscore the transformative power of research in improving the lives of individuals with rare diseases and the importance of continued investment in this field. As we proceed through the subsequent chapters, we will explore additional dimensions of rare diseases, including patient advocacy, support networks, and the journey towards better treatment options and improved quality of life.

5

Chapter 5: Patient Advocacy and Support Groups

The journey of individuals and families affected by rare diseases is often fraught with challenges, and patient advocacy groups and support networks play a crucial role in providing assistance, raising awareness, and driving progress. In this chapter, we will explore the power of patient advocacy and the invaluable support offered by various organizations.

The Power of Patient Advocacy:

Patient advocacy is a driving force behind advancements in the understanding and management of rare diseases. This section will delve into the impact of patient advocacy, including:

- How advocacy efforts have shaped rare disease research and policy.
- The role of patients and their families in raising awareness.
- Successful examples of patient-led initiatives and movements.

Support Organizations and Networks:

Numerous organizations and networks have emerged to support individuals with rare diseases and their families. These groups provide a lifeline, offering emotional support, information, and resources. This section will cover:

- The diverse range of rare disease support organizations.

- The services and resources they provide, from educational materials to financial assistance.

- The role of these organizations in connecting individuals and fostering a sense of community.

Real-Life Patient Stories:

Patient stories provide a profound insight into the daily challenges, triumphs, and resilience of those affected by rare diseases. This section will feature real-life accounts, including:

- Stories of individuals and families navigating the complexities of rare diseases.

- The role of advocacy and support networks in these personal narratives.

- How patient stories can inspire and inform others within the rare disease community.

Advocating for Policy Change:

Patient advocacy often extends beyond emotional support and awareness raising to advocating for policy change. Individuals and organizations lobby for increased funding, better healthcare access, and improved research efforts. This section will explore:

- The impact of rare disease policy advocacy at the local, national, and international levels.

- The achievements and ongoing efforts in influencing healthcare policies.

- The importance of collaboration between patient advocates, researchers, and policymakers.

Global Rare Disease Day:

Global Rare Disease Day is a key event in the rare disease community, serving as a platform to raise awareness and unite individuals, organizations, and policymakers in support of those affected by rare diseases. This section will discuss:

- The history and significance of Global Rare Disease Day.

- Events and activities held worldwide to mark the day.

- The collective impact of a global call for action in the rare disease community.

This chapter will underscore the profound significance of patient advocacy and support networks in the rare disease landscape. Through the stories, dedication, and collaborative efforts of individuals and organizations, rare diseases gain the attention, resources, and support they deserve. As we progress through the subsequent chapters, we will explore the specific challenges of accessing treatment and the development of orphan drugs, as well as the impact of rare diseases on mental health and the role of caregivers and families.

6

Chapter 6: Access to Treatment and Orphan Drugs

Access to appropriate treatment is a critical aspect of the rare disease journey, often marked by challenges due to the scarcity of effective therapies. In this chapter, we will explore the specific challenges individuals with rare diseases face in accessing treatment, the development of orphan drugs, and the efforts to improve access.

Orphan Drug Development:
Orphan drugs are medications specifically developed to treat rare diseases. This section will delve into the development process, including:
- The incentives and regulatory pathways that encourage orphan drug development.
- The role of pharmaceutical companies, academia, and government agencies.
- Examples of successful orphan drugs that have transformed the lives of individuals with rare diseases.

Challenges in Accessing Treatment:
Access to treatment for rare diseases presents a unique set of challenges, including high costs, limited availability, and insurance coverage issues. This

section will address:

- The financial burden of rare disease treatments and the impact on families.

- The importance of insurance coverage, including Medicaid and Medicare.

- The role of patient advocacy in improving access to treatments.

Advocating for Better Access:

Patient advocacy groups and rare disease organizations often lead the charge in advocating for better access to treatment options. This section will explore:

- How advocacy efforts have influenced policy changes to improve access.

- The importance of a patient-centered approach in healthcare decision-making.

- Case studies illustrating successful advocacy initiatives that have broadened access to treatments.

Global Efforts in Rare Disease Treatment:

Rare diseases are a global challenge, and international collaboration is essential to ensure equitable access to treatments. This section will highlight:

- Global initiatives and organizations focused on improving access to rare disease treatments.

- The role of global health diplomacy in addressing disparities in access.

- The impact of sharing best practices and knowledge across borders.

Future Directions in Rare Disease Treatment:

The landscape of rare disease treatment is continuously evolving, with promising innovations on the horizon. This section will explore:

- Emerging technologies and therapies, such as gene therapy and RNA-based treatments.

- The potential for personalized medicine to tailor treatments to an individual's unique genetic profile.

- The importance of research and innovation in addressing unmet treatment needs for rare diseases.

This chapter underscores the importance of addressing the challenges of accessing treatment for rare diseases and the role of orphan drug development in transforming the lives of affected individuals. As we continue through the subsequent chapters, we will explore the impact of rare diseases on mental health, the support networks available for caregivers and families, and the legislative and policy initiatives that shape the rare disease landscape.

7

Chapter 7: Rare Diseases and Mental Health

Living with a rare disease can take a significant toll on an individual's mental health and emotional well-being. This chapter delves into the psychological and emotional challenges faced by those affected by rare diseases and the support systems in place to address these issues.

Coping with Uncertainty:

Individuals diagnosed with rare diseases often face a high degree of uncertainty. This section explores how the unpredictability of the condition, misdiagnoses, and unanswered questions can affect mental health. Topics include:

- The emotional impact of a rare disease diagnosis.
- Strategies for coping with uncertainty and managing stress.
- The role of patient support networks and mental health professionals.

Psychological and Emotional Challenges:

Rare diseases can lead to a range of psychological and emotional challenges, including anxiety, depression, and social isolation. This section discusses:

- The emotional impact on individuals and their families.
- Stigmatization and the feeling of being misunderstood.

- Coping strategies and the importance of open communication.

Support for Mental Well-being:
Mental health support is crucial for individuals living with rare diseases. This section outlines the resources and support systems available, including:
- Psychosocial support from healthcare providers.
- Support groups and counseling services.
- The role of family and friends in providing emotional support.

The Importance of Resilience:
Resilience is a key factor in coping with the challenges of living with a rare disease. This section explores:
- The stories of individuals who have demonstrated remarkable resilience.
- Strategies for building and nurturing resilience.
- The role of positive psychology in promoting mental well-being.

Advocacy for Mental Health:
Advocacy efforts within the rare disease community extend to mental health support. This section highlights the importance of advocacy in:
- Raising awareness about the mental health challenges faced by individuals with rare diseases.
- Advocating for better mental health services and resources.
- The impact of patient-led initiatives in promoting mental health awareness.

This chapter emphasizes the psychological and emotional challenges often encountered by individuals living with rare diseases and the importance of addressing mental health concerns within the rare disease community. As we continue through the subsequent chapters, we will explore the vital role of caregivers and family support, legislative and policy initiatives, and the evolving role of technology in rare disease management.

8

Chapter 8: Caregivers and Family Support

The impact of rare diseases extends beyond the individuals affected; it profoundly influences the lives of their caregivers and families. In this chapter, we will explore the crucial role that caregivers play and the support systems available to assist them in their caregiving journey.

The Impact on Families:

A diagnosis of a rare disease has far-reaching consequences for families. This section delves into how rare diseases affect family dynamics, including:

- Emotional and financial challenges faced by families.
- The stress of caregiving and the need for balance.
- Strategies for fostering resilience and unity within the family.

Caregiving Challenges:

Caregivers of individuals with rare diseases face unique challenges due to the complexities and uncertainties of these conditions. This section discusses:

- The physical and emotional toll of caregiving.
- Balancing caregiving responsibilities with work and personal life.
- The importance of self-care for caregivers.

Resources for Caregivers:

A range of resources and support networks are available to assist caregivers

in their role. This section highlights the various forms of support, including:
- Support groups for caregivers.
- Educational resources to enhance caregiving skills.
- Respite care services to provide caregivers with temporary relief.

Advocacy for Caregivers:

Caregivers are often strong advocates for individuals with rare diseases. This section explores how caregivers can play a crucial role in advocacy efforts by:
- Advocating for policies that support caregivers.
- Raising awareness about the needs and challenges of caregiving.
- Collaborating with patient advocacy groups to drive change.

Inspirational Caregiver Stories:

This section includes real-life stories of caregivers who have shown remarkable dedication and resilience in their caregiving journey. These stories inspire and illustrate the profound impact of caregivers on the lives of individuals with rare diseases.

This chapter shines a light on the often-overlooked role of caregivers and the challenges they face in caring for loved ones with rare diseases. It underscores the importance of providing caregivers with the support and resources they need to navigate their caregiving responsibilities effectively. As we progress through the subsequent chapters, we will explore legislative and policy initiatives, the role of technology in rare disease management, and the global collaboration that is shaping the rare disease landscape.

9

Chapter 9: Legislative and Policy Initiatives

Legislation and policies play a critical role in addressing the unique challenges faced by individuals with rare diseases. In this chapter, we will explore the legislative and policy initiatives at the local, national, and international levels that impact the rare disease community.

Rare Disease Policies Worldwide:

Rare disease policies and initiatives vary from one country to another. This section will provide an overview of the landscape, including:
- Examples of countries with well-established rare disease policies.
- The development of national plans and strategies.
- Challenges in implementing and enforcing rare disease policies.

Advocating for Policy Change:

Patient advocacy groups and individuals affected by rare diseases are often at the forefront of advocating for policy change. This section delves into:
- The role of advocacy in influencing policymakers and lawmakers.
- Successful case studies of advocacy efforts leading to policy change.
- The importance of patient voices in shaping rare disease policies.

Orphan Drug Legislation:

Orphan drug legislation is a crucial component of the rare disease policy framework. This section explores the development and impact of orphan drug legislation, including:
- The incentives and protections provided by orphan drug laws.
- Examples of successful orphan drug programs around the world.
- The challenges and criticisms associated with orphan drug policies.

Global Collaboration in Rare Disease Policy:

Rare diseases are a global challenge, and collaboration at the international level is essential. This section highlights:
- International organizations and initiatives focused on rare disease policy.
- The importance of sharing best practices and knowledge across borders.
- Case studies of successful global collaboration efforts.

Access to Care and Treatment:

Policy initiatives are instrumental in ensuring individuals with rare diseases have access to quality care and treatment. This section discusses:
- The impact of healthcare reform and insurance coverage.
- The role of policy in reducing healthcare disparities.
- The importance of patient-centered care in rare disease policy.

This chapter underscores the significance of legislative and policy initiatives in addressing the unique needs and challenges of individuals with rare diseases. As we continue through the subsequent chapters, we will explore the role of technology in rare disease management, global collaboration, and the stories of hope and resilience that inspire individuals in the rare disease community.

10

Chapter 10: The Role of Technology in Rare Disease Management

Technology has become an increasingly valuable tool in the management and care of individuals with rare diseases. This chapter explores the innovative ways in which technology is transforming the landscape of rare disease management, from diagnosis to treatment and support.

Telemedicine and Remote Support:

Telemedicine has become a game-changer in the rare disease community, offering individuals access to specialized healthcare regardless of their geographical location. This section discusses:
- The role of telemedicine in rare disease diagnosis and consultations.
- Remote monitoring and support for individuals with chronic rare diseases.
- The benefits and challenges of telehealth in rare disease care.

Wearable Devices and Tracking:

Wearable technology has revolutionized the way individuals and healthcare providers monitor and manage rare diseases. This section explores:
- Wearable devices that track vital signs, symptoms, and medication adherence.

- The potential for early detection and intervention through wearables.

- Privacy and security considerations in using wearable technology.

Tele-Rehabilitation and Physical Therapy:

Rare diseases often necessitate physical therapy and rehabilitation. Tele-rehabilitation offers innovative solutions for individuals who may have limited mobility. This section discusses:

- The role of tele-rehabilitation in rare disease management.

- Virtual physical therapy sessions and exercise programs.

- The advantages of tele-rehabilitation for both patients and healthcare providers.

Supportive Apps and Platforms:

A variety of mobile apps and online platforms cater to the unique needs of individuals with rare diseases. This section highlights:

- Apps that help individuals track symptoms, medication, and appointments.

- Online communities and social platforms for rare disease support and information.

- The potential for digital health tools to improve quality of life.

Data Analytics and Research:

Technology plays a vital role in accelerating rare disease research through data analytics and artificial intelligence. This section explores:

- How AI is used to identify potential drug candidates.

- The importance of data sharing and analysis in rare disease research.

- Examples of technological advancements in genomics and proteomics.

This chapter emphasizes the transformative power of technology in rare disease management, from improving access to care through telemedicine to enhancing daily life through wearable devices and supportive apps. As we continue through the subsequent chapters, we will explore global collaboration, inspiring stories of hope and resilience, and the future directions in rare disease research and care.

11

Chapter 11: Global Collaboration and Future Prospects

The rare disease community faces unique challenges that require global collaboration and innovative approaches. In this chapter, we will explore the international efforts aimed at addressing rare diseases and the future prospects for research, advocacy, and support.

International Research Efforts:

Rare diseases know no borders, and international research collaborations have become crucial in advancing our understanding and treatment of these conditions. This section discusses:

- The importance of sharing research findings and resources across nations.

- Collaborative initiatives, such as the International Rare Diseases Research Consortium (IRDiRC).

- The impact of global research efforts on rare disease discoveries.

Global Health Diplomacy:

Global health diplomacy plays a significant role in advocating for the needs of the rare disease community on the international stage. This section explores:

- How diplomacy is used to address global health challenges, including rare diseases.

- The role of intergovernmental organizations and diplomatic efforts in raising awareness and driving policy change.

- The significance of advocating for rare diseases as a global public health concern.

Future Directions in Rare Disease Research:

The landscape of rare disease research is continuously evolving, offering new prospects and opportunities. This section highlights:

- Emerging technologies, such as gene editing, CRISPR-Cas9, and RNA-based therapies.

- The potential for precision medicine to tailor treatments to an individual's genetic profile.

- The role of AI, big data, and patient-driven research in shaping the future of rare disease research.

Global Collaboration in Advocacy:

Rare disease advocacy is not limited to a single country, and international advocacy efforts are crucial in addressing the collective needs of the rare disease community. This section discusses:

- The importance of advocating for global rare disease policies.

- International rare disease awareness campaigns and events.

- The collective impact of a global call to action in the rare disease community.

The Importance of Rare Disease Stories:

The stories of individuals and families affected by rare diseases continue to inspire and inform the rare disease community. This section emphasizes:

- The power of patient narratives in advocating for change.

- How patient stories can influence research and policy.

- The importance of preserving and sharing rare disease stories for future generations.

This chapter underscores the significance of global collaboration in addressing rare diseases and the promising future prospects for research, advocacy, and support. As we continue through the subsequent chapters, we will explore the inspirational stories of hope and resilience within the rare disease community, the need for policies that support rare disease care and research, and the journey towards a brighter future for those affected by these conditions.

12

Chapter 12: Stories of Hope and Resilience

Amid the challenges and complexities of living with rare diseases, stories of hope and resilience abound. This chapter serves as a testament to the strength, determination, and triumph of individuals and families within the rare disease community.

Inspirational Patient Journeys:

This section shares real-life stories of individuals who have faced the hurdles of rare diseases with courage and resilience. It highlights their journeys, struggles, and achievements. These stories illustrate the resilience of the human spirit and inspire others on their own rare disease journey.

Triumphs Against the Odds:

Despite the challenges, individuals with rare diseases have achieved remarkable milestones. This section showcases examples of extraordinary achievements, such as educational accomplishments, artistic endeavors, and advocacy efforts. These triumphs emphasize the potential and determination of individuals with rare diseases.

The Importance of Hope:

Hope is a powerful force in the rare disease community. This section discusses the significance of hope and its role in driving progress. It explores how hope can sustain individuals, families, and researchers through difficult times and keep them focused on finding solutions and making a difference.

Resilience in the Face of Adversity:

Rare diseases demand resilience from those who are affected. This section explores the resilience of individuals and their families in the face of adversity. It highlights the strength they draw from their support networks, their personal determination, and their ability to adapt to life's challenges.

The Influence of Collective Resilience:

The rare disease community is a network of individuals and organizations that support one another. This section discusses the collective resilience of the community and how individuals, families, and advocacy groups work together to drive progress, awareness, and positive change.

This final chapter emphasizes the remarkable stories of hope and resilience that inspire the rare disease community and remind us of the remarkable human spirit. It serves as a testament to the strength of individuals and families living with rare diseases, the unwavering dedication of researchers and healthcare professionals, and the transformative impact of advocacy efforts. These stories offer hope for a brighter future for all those affected by rare diseases.